SHAMBHALA POCKET LIBRARY

AFTER IKKYŪ

and Other Poems

_____

Jim Harrison

SHAMBHALA · Boulder · 2018

SHAMBHALA PUBLICATIONS, INC.
4720 Walnut Street
Boulder, Colorado 80301
www.shambhala.com

9 8 7 6 5 4 3 2

Printed in the United States of America

♾ This edition is printed on acid-free paper that meets the
American National Standards Institute z39.48 Standard.
♺ Shambhala Publications makes every effort to print on recycled
paper. For more information please visit us at www.shambhala.com.

Shambhala Publications is distributed worldwide by
Penguin Random House, Inc., and its subsidiaries.

THE LIBRARY OF CONGRESS catalogues the previous edition
OF THIS BOOK AS FOLLOWS:
Harrison, Jim, 1937–
After Ikkyū and other poems/Jim Harrison.—1st ed.
p. pm.
ISBN 1-57062-218-3 (alk. paper)
ISBN 1-57062-299-X (cloth)
ISBN 978-1-61180-621-2 (Shambhala Pocket Library)
1. Zen poetry, American. 1. Title.
PS3558.A67A69 1996 96-11501
811'.54—dc20   CIP

CONTENTS

PREFACE

I began my Zen studies and practice well over twenty years ago in a state of rapacious and self-congratulatory spiritual greed. I immediately set about reading hundreds of books on the subject, almost all contemporary and informed by an earnest mediocrity. There was no more self-referential organism alive than myself, a potato that didn't know it was a potato.

Naturally the years have passed quickly, if not brutishly. I practiced because I value life and this seems the best way for me to get at the heart of the matter. We are more than dying flies in a shithouse, though we are that, too. There are hundreds of ways to tip off a cushion and only one way to sit there. Zen is the vehicle of reality, and I see almost as much of it in Wordsworth as I do in Ch'an texts. As I've said before, it's easy to mistake the plumbing for the river. We in the West are prone to ignore our own literary traditions, while in the East Zennists were industriously syncretic, gathering poetry, Confucius, and Taoism to their breasts. There is scarcely a better koan than Ahab before the whiteness of a whale who sees a different ocean from each side of its massive head.

The sequence *After Ikkyū* was occasioned when Jack Turner passed along to me *The Record of Tungshan* and the new *Master Yunmen*, edited by Urs App. It was a dark period, and I spent a great deal of time with the books. They rattled me loose from the oppressive, poleaxed state of distraction we count as worldly success. But then we are not fueled by piths and gists but by practice—which is Yunmen's unshakable point, among a thousand other harrowing ones. I was born a baby, what are these hundred suits of clothes I'm wearing?

Of course, the reader should be mindful that I'm a poet, and we tend to err on the side that life is more than it appears rather than less. I do not remotely consider myself a "Zen Buddhist," as that is too ineptly convenient and a specific barrier for one whose life-long obsession has been his art rather than his religion. Someone like Robert Aitken Roshi is a Zen Buddhist. I'm still a fool. Early on in my teens I suffocated myself with Protestant theology and am mindful, in Coleridge's terms, that, like spiders, we spin webs of deceit out of our big hanging asses, whether with Jesus or the Buddha.

But still practice is accretive, and who has opened doors for me like Zen creatures—Peter Matthiessen,

Gary Snyder, Kobun Chino Sensei, Bob Watkins, Dan Gerber, and Jack Turner, to name a few prominent ones?

It doesn't really matter if these poems are thought of as slightly soiled dharma gates or just plain poems. They'll live or die by their own specific density, flowers for the void. The poems were written within the discreet interval described so poignantly by Tung-shan:

Earnestly avoid seeking without,
Lest it recede far from you.
Today I am walking alone,
Yet everywhere I meet him.
He is now no other than myself,
But I am not now him.
It must be understood in this way
In order to merge with Suchness.

To write a poem you must first create a pen that will write what you want to say. For better or worse, this is the work of a lifetime.

AFTER IKKYŪ

for Jack Turner

I

Our minds buzz like bees
but not the bees' minds.
It's just wings not heart
they say, moving to another flower.

2

The well pit is beneath where the pump shed burned
years ago with a living roar, a fire lion. Down
in the pit, charred timbers, green grass, one burdock,
a vernal pool where frogs live trapped in a universe.

3

I've wasted too much moonlight.
Breast beating. I'll waste no more moonlight,
the moon bullied by clouds drifts west
in her imponderable arc, snared for a half
hour among the wet leaves in the birdbath.

4

After thirty years of work
I take three months off
and wait for the mirror's image to fade.
These chess pieces, slippery with blood.

5

Time eats us alive.
On my birthday yesterday
I was only one day older
though I began 10 million eons ago
as a single cell in the old mud homestead.

6

Shōjū sat all night in the graveyard
among wolves who sniffed his Adam's apple.
First light moving in the air
he arose, peed, and ate breakfast.

7

With each shot
he killed the self
until there was no one left
to bring home the bacon.

8

One part of the brain attacks another,
seven parts attack nine parts,
then the war begins to subside
from lack of ammunition,
but out there I know the mules are bringing
fresh supplies from over the mountain.

9

Poor little blind boy, lost in the storm
where should he go to be without harm?
For starters, the dickhead should get a life.
Once I had a moment of absolute balance
while dancing with my sick infant daughter
to Merle Haggard. The blind boy died in the storm
with fresh frozen laughter hot on his lips.

Our pup is gravely ill.
She's her own pup too,
first in her own line.
How great thou art o god,
save her, please, the same cry
in every throat. May I live forever.

11

At Hard Luck Ranch the tea is hot,
the sky's dark blue. Behind me
the jaguar skin from the jaguar
who died so long ago from a bullet
while perched on a calf's back,
tells me the same old story.

12

Not here and now but now and here.
If you don't know the difference
is a matter of life and death, get down
naked on bare knees in the snow
and study the ticking of your watch.

13

The hound I've known for three years
trots down the mountain road
with a nod at me, pretending he knows
what he's doing miles from home
on a sunlit morning. He's headed
for a kind of place he hasn't quite found yet
and might not recognize when he gets there.

14

At the strip club in Lincoln, Nebraska,
she said, "I'm the Princess of Shalimar."
Doubtless, I thought, at a loss for words
but not images, the air moist but without
the promise of a rain. She's not bending
pinkly like a pretzel but a body.
At this age, my first bona fide royalty.

15

Way up a sandy draw in the foothills
of the Whetstone Mountains I found cougar
tracks so fresh damp sand was still
trickling in from the edges. For some reason
I knelt and sniffed them, quite sure
I was being watched by a living rock
in the vast, heat-blurred landscape.

16

I went to Tucson and it gave
me a headache. I don't know how.
Everyone's a cousin in this world.
I drove down a road of enormous houses
that encompass many toilets. Down hallways,
leaping left or right, you can crap at will.
A mile away a dead Mexican child slept
out in the desert on the wrong side of a mattress.

17

Up at the Hard Luck Ranch
there's a pyracantha bush full of red berries
right outside my study window.
In December after seven hard frosts
the birds arrive to eat the fermented berries.
The birds get drunk and unwary in this saloon
and the barn cats have a bird feast.
A phainopepla landed on my head, shrieking
when my eyebrow moved, booze on its bird breath.

My zabuton doubles as a dog bed. Rose sleeps
there, full to the fur with *mu*. Glanced in
on a moonlight night; her slight white figure coiled
on the green cushion, shaking with quail dreams.
Sensing me, an eye opens, single tail wag. Back to
    sleep.
When she's awake, she's so awake I'm ashamed
of my own warm water dance, my sitting too long at
    the fire.

19

Time gets foreshortened late at night.
Jesus died a few days ago, my father
and sister just before lunch. At dawn
I fished, then hoed corn. Married at midmorning,
wept for a second. We were poor momentarily
for a decade. Within a few minutes I made
a round trip to Paris. I drank and ate during a parade
in my room. One blink, Red Mountain's still there.

20

More lion prints in our creekbed.
Right now in the light, cool rain at midnight,
coyotes. Skunk stink laden in mist.
Hidden moon, I don't want to go home yet.
Older, the flavors of earth are more delicious.

21

Just like today eternity is accomplished
in split seconds. I read that Old Nieh
in the wilderness vastness trained a mountain
tiger to carry his firewood. A black hole the size
of 300 billion suns is gobbling up the M87
galaxy because astronomers gave it a boring name.
Time passed in sitting begs mercy from the clock.

22

Out in an oak-lined field down the road
I again saw time, trotting in circles
around the far edges. The dog didn't notice
though she's usually more attentive. She lost
the Christmas watch I gave her
in a mountain canyon at the edge of earth.

23

It certainly wasn't fish who discovered water
or birds the air. Men built houses in part
out of embarrassment by the stars
and raised their children on trivialities
because they had butchered the god within
     themselves.
The politician standing on the church steps thrives
within the grandeur of this stupidity,
a burnt out lamp who never imagined the sun.

24

The monk is eighty-seven. There's no fat
left on his feet to defend against stones.
He forgot his hat, larger in recent years.
By a creek he sees a woman he saw fifty summers
before, somehow still a girl to him. Once again his
    hands
tremble when she gives him a tin cup of water.

25

Talked to the God of Hosts about the Native American
situation and he said everything's a matter of time,
that though it's small comfort the ghosts have already
nearly destroyed us with the ugliness we've become,
that in a few hidden glades in North America
half-human bears still dance in imperfect circles.

This adobe is no protection against the flossy
sweep of stars that in recent nights burn pinprick
holes in my skin, mostly in the skull despite my orange
stocking cap, hunter's orange so you won't get shot
by other hunters, a color the stars readily ignore
with beams of white fire. O stars, you forsaken suns.

27

I confess that here and there in my life
there is a vision of a great brown toad
leaking words of love and doom through his skin,
excrescences that would kill anyone, given time,
his words tinged as they are with the shapes
of death, one drumbeat, a heartbeat, the skins
of gods a rug spread beneath our feet.

Lin-chi says, having thrown away your head so long
ago, you go on and on looking for it in the wrong
places. The head's future can be studied in a spadeful
of dirt. The delightful girl I loved 40 years back
now weighs, according to necrologists, 30 lbs. net.
Why does she still swim in the eddy in the river's
    bend?

29

The four seasons, the ten oaths, the nine colors, three
    vowels
that stretch forth their paltry hands to the seven
    flavors
and the one money, the official parody of prayer.
Up on this mountain, stumbling on talus, on the
    north face
there is snow, and on the south, buds of pink flowers.

30

It is difficult to imagine the wordless conversations
between Jesus and Buddha going on this very moment.
These androgynous blood brothers demand our
    imagination.
They could ask Shakespeare and Mozart to write
    words
and music, and perhaps a dozen others, but they've
    done so.
The vast asteroid on its way toward L.A. goes
    unmentioned.

31

Come down to earth! Get your head out of your ass!
Get your head out of the clouds! Stop mooning
    around!
Pay attention. Get to work on time.
Time and tide that wait for no man willingly
pause for the barearmed girl brushing her hair
in a brown pickup truck on a summer evening.

32

If that bald head gets you closer to Buddha
try chemotherapy. Your hair drops casually to the floor,
eyes widen until the skull aches, the heart beats like
Thumper's foot. Heaven's near at every second.
Now you've become that lamb you refused to eat.

33

I haven't accepted the fact that I'll never understand
the universe that I saw clearly for the first time
from our roof at nineteen in miniature kensho.
We belonged to each other. Love at first sight,
notwithstanding the child who stared in fear
at the northern lights and noted the milky way's
      convulsive
drift. A lone star perched on the mountain's
saddle now brings tears of doubt.

34

It wasn't until the sixth century that the Christians
decided animals weren't part of the kingdom of
    heaven.
Hoof, wing, and paw can't put money in the collection
    plate.
These lunatic shit-brained fools excluded our beloved
    creatures.
Theologians and accountants, the same thing really,
    join
evangelists on television, shadowy as viruses.

35

Everywhere I go I study the scars on earth's face,
including rivers and lakes. I'm not playing God
but assessing intent. In the Patagonia Mountains
you think, "small mines, pathetic deaths." In Cabeza
    Prieta
men boiled in their own blood, ground temperature
    170°F.
Contrails of earthen scar tissue, creeks stink of sulfur.
Gold & copper to buy the horse that died, the woman
    who left.

36

Ten thousand pointless equations left just after dawn,
the city's air heavy with the fat of countless dieters.
Saw Ummon strolling down Wilshire with Yunmen,
unperturbed, disappearing into each other, emerging
with laughter. Saw thirty-three green, waking parrots
watch a single black cat raising the dew as she walked
across the golf course, the first one to the seventh tee.

37

Beware, o wanderer, the road is walking too,
said Rilke one day to no one in particular
as good poets everywhere address the six directions.
If you can't bow, you're dead meat. You'll break
like uncooked spaghetti. Listen to the gods.
They're shouting in your ear every second.

38

Who remembers Wang Che, "the real human like
multiplied sunlight"? No one, of course
but his words are a lamp for any fool's feet.
He can't stop you from drowning, but he can keep
you out of the boat. This water's meant for careful
     wading,
but imagining my ears are gills, I still dive there at
     night.

39

In the next installment I'll give you Crazy Horse and
    Anne Frank,
their conversation as recorded by Matthew of Gospel
    fame,
who was wont, as all scriveners, to add a bit of this
    and that.
God is terse. The earth's proper scripture could be
    carried
on a three-by-five card if we weren't drunk on our
    own blood.

40

Walking the lakeshore at first moonlight I can see
feathers, stones, smooth spars, seaweed,
and the doe washed up from the Manitous two
    days ago
has been nearly eaten by the coyotes and ravens.
I poke my stick in the moon's watery face, then
    apologize.

41

Home again. It looked different for a moment.
The birds, while not decrepit, flew slower.
The dogs wagged and licked their greetings,
then went back to sleep, unmindful of airplanes.
The new moon said either gather yourself for your last
decade, or slow down big pony, fat snake shed another
   skin.

42

Inside people fear the outside; outside, the in.
But then I'm always halfway in or out the door,
most comfortable and at home in this fear,
knowing that falling is best for my nature.
Backwards works well, or gathered for the leeward
pitch, imitate the sea in perfect balance in her
    torment.

43

The world is wrenched on her pivot, shivering.
    Politicians
and preachers are standing on their heads, shitting
out of their mouths. Lucky for us Stephen Mitchell
has restored the Gospels, returning the Jesus
I imagined at fourteen, offering up my clumsy life
in a damp shroud of hormones. Most of all he said
"pay attention," Buddha nodding from the wings.

44

The dawn of the day we arrived Abel Murrietta
saw a big mountain lion sitting behind our gate.
This is not an omen but a lion, the borderguard
athwart our time in the chaos of the wild, the other
that draws us to speechlessness, the lion behind
    the gate
turning her head, flowing up the mountainside to sit,
gazing at twilight at the *casita*, creekbed, our shared
    thickets.

45

The sound of the dog's paw steps move away
at the precise speed of his shadow. Nothing is blurred.
The bullet tumbled toward the girl's head at 1250 feet
per second. She wasn't the president, you say,
too young for politics. Despite theological gooseshit
the gods don't keep time in light years. We're slowed
to the brutality of clocks. Listen to the alarm.

    Wake up.

46

Sometimes a toothpick is the most important thing,
others, a roll of toilet paper. If you forget red wine
and garlic you'll become honky, new age incense
dressed in invisible taffeta. Eat meat or not,
try weighing your virtue on that bathroom scale
right after you crap and shower. You're just a tree
that grows shit, not fruit. Your high horse is dead meat.

47

The girl's bottom is beautiful as Peacock's dancing
    bear
who is 70 miles from any of our fevered instruments.
Neither girl or bear utter a word to the world in
    between
in its careless sump. The Virgin said zip to the
    Garrison.
If you can't dance without music jump into an icy lake.
Think of the brown girl at the A&W Root Beer stand.

48

It was Monday morning for most of the world
and my heart nearly exploded according
to my digital high blood pressure machine,
telling me I don't want to work anymore
as the highest paid coal miner on earth.
I want to stay up on the surface and help the heron
who's been having trouble with his creekbed landings.
He's getting old and I wonder where he'll be when
   he dies.

49

Jesus wants me for a sunbeam, I sang in Sunday
school a lifetime ago, way up in cold country
where there wasn't much sun. A sunbeam in winter
made one recoil and everyone stared mutely upward.
The bogeyman still smiles, now from a glass
of whiskey, then from a farmhouse root cellar.
A little boy bred this man with no thought of the
    future.

50

If I'm not mistaken, everyone seems to go back
to where they came from, ending up right
where they began. Our beloved cat died today.
She liked to sit on my head during zazen
back when she was a child. I bow to her magnificence
beside which all churches and temples are privy holes.

51

A lovely woman in Minnesota owned a 100-year-old
    horse,
actually 37, but in horse years that's at least a 100.
In the third grade I read there were eleven surviving
Civil War veterans. Under the photo captions it said
they were mostly drummer boys. Now both
horse and veterans are dead, the woman married, rid
of her binding sweetheart horse. I know these peculiar
things because I'm Jim, at the right place, the right
    time.

52

Once and for all there's no genetic virtue.
Our cherubic baldy flounces around, fresh out of
    Boulder,
in black robes, Japanese words quick on his tongue.
World War II nearly destroyed my family, so I ask
him to learn Chinese. He understands I'm a fool.
Then over a gallon of wine we agree there's no
    language
for such matters, no happiness outside consciousness.
    Drink.

53

Sam got tired of the way life fudged the big issues,
drank a quart of vodka, shot himself in the parking lot
of the tavern. How could a friend do this to himself?
It was relatively easy. Anyone can do it in a blink.
We won't look for black bears again out by Barfield
    Lakes.
Some don't go up in smoke but are strangled off
    the earth.

54

This morning I felt strong and jaunty in my mail order
Israeli commando trousers. Up at Hard Luck Ranch I
  spoke
to the ravens in baritone, fed the cats with manly
  gestures.
Acacia thorns can't penetrate these mighty pants.
  Then out
by the corral the infant pup began to weep,
  abandoned.
In an instant I became another of earth's billion sad
  mothers.

55

I once thought that life's what's left over after
I extricate myself from the mess. I was writing a poem
about paying attention and microwaved a hot dog
so hot it burned a beet-red hole in the roof of my
      mouth.
Lucrezia Borgia got shit on her fingers by not paying
attention. Chanting a sutra, the monk stepped fatally
on the viper's tail. Every gun is loaded and cocked.

I've emerged from the seven going on eight divorces
that have surrounded me for three years. I kept on
     saying,
look at me, I'm not wise. I've advised seven suicides.
No one's separate. Our legs grow into the horse's
     body.
You've ridden each other too long to get off now.
You can make a clean getaway only if you cut off your
     heads.
All in vain. Life won't get simple until our mind does.
Embrace the great emptiness, say again, I don't do
     divorces.

57

Took my own life because I was permanently crippled,
put on backwards, the repairs eating up money and
    time.
For fifty-seven years I've had it all wrong
until I studied the other side of the mirror.
No birth before death. The other way around.
How pleasant to get off a horse in the middle of
    a lake.

OTHER POEMS

The Davenport Lunar Eclipse

Overlooking the Mississippi
I never thought I'd get this old.
It was mostly my confusion about time
and the moon, and seeing the lovely way
homely old men treat their homely old women
in Nebraska and Iowa, the lunch time
touch over green Jell-O with pineapple
and fried "fish rectangles" for $2.95.
When I passed Des Moines the radio said
there were long lines to see the entire cow
sculpted out of butter. The earth is right smack
between the sun and the moon, the black waitress
told me at the Salty Pelican on the waterfront,
home from wild Houston to nurse her sick dad.
My good eye is burning up from fatigue
as it squints up above the Mississippi
where the moon is losing its edge to black.
It likely doesn't know what's happening to it,
I thought, pressed down to my meal and wine
by a fresh load of incomprehension.
My grandma lived in Davenport in the 1890s
just after Wounded Knee, a signal event,
the beginning of America's *Sickness unto Death*.
I'd like to nurse my father back to health
he's been dead thirty years, I said

to the waitress who agreed. That's why she
came home, she said, you only got one.
Now I find myself at fifty-one in Davenport
and drop the issue right into the Mississippi
where it is free to swim with the moon's
    reflection.
At the bar there are two girls of incomprehensible
    beauty
for the time being, as Swedish as my Grandma,
speaking in bad grammar as they listen to a band
of middle-aged Swede saxophonists braying
"Bye-Bye Blackbird" over and over, with a clumsy
but specific charm. The girls fail to notice me—
perhaps I should give them the thousand dollars
in my wallet but I've forgot just how.
I feel pleasantly old and stupid, deciding
not to worry about who I am but how I spend
my days, until I tear in the weak places
like a thin, worn sheet. Back in my room
I can't hear the river passing like time,
or the moon emerging from the shadow of earth,
but I can see the water that never repeats itself.
It's very difficult to look at the World
and into your heart at the same time.
In between, a life has passed.

Coyote No. 1

Just before dark
watched coyote take a crap
on rock out cropping,
flexing hips (no time off)
swiveled owl-like to see
in all six directions:
sky above
earth below,
points of compass
in two half circles.
There.
And there is no distance.
He knows the dreamer
that dreams his dreams.

Time Suite

Just seven weeks ago in Paris
I read Chuang-tzu in my dreams
and remembered once again
we are only here for a moment,
not very wild mushrooms,
those cartoon creatures that are blown apart
and only think they are put back together,
housepets within a housefire of impermanence.
In this cold cellar we see light
without knowing it is out of reach;
not to be owned but earned
moment by moment.
But still at dawn
in the middle of Paris' heart
there was a crow I spoke to
on the cornice far above my window.
It is the crow from home
that cawed above the immense
gaunt bear eating sweet pea vines
and wild strawberries.
Today in the garden of Luxembourg
I passed through clumps of frozen vines
and saw a man in a bulletproof
glass house guarding stone,
a girl in the pink suit
of an unknown animal,

lovers nursing at each other's mouths.
I know that at my deathbed's urging
there'll be no clocks and I'll cry out
for eat not light.

This lady is stuck
on an elevator
shuddering
between the planets.

If life has passed this quickly,
a millennium is not all that long.
At fourteen
my sex fantasies
about Lucrezia Borgia:
I loved her name, the image
of her *renascimento* undies,
her feet in the stirrups
of a golden saddle.
She's gone now
these many years.

Dad told me that we have time
so that everything won't happen at once.
For instance, deaths are spread out.
It would be real hard on people
if all the deaths for the year
occurred the same day.

Lemuribus vertebrates,
ossibus inter-tenebras—
"For the vertebrate ghosts,
for the bones among the darknesses."
Quoted the great Bringhurst,
who could have conquered Manhattan
and returned it to the Natives,
who might have continued dancing
on the rocky sward.

The stillness
of dog shadows.

Here is time.
In the crotch of limbs
the cow's skull grew
into the tree
and birds nested in the mouth
year after year.
Human blood still fertilizes
the crops of Yurp.
The humus owns names:
Fred and Ted from old Missouri,
Cedric and Basil from Cornwall,
Heinz and Hans from Stuttgart,
Fyodor and Gretel in final embrace
beside raped Sylvie,
clod to clod.

The actual speed of life
is so much slower
we could have lived
exactly seven times as long
as we did.

These calendars
with pussy photos
send us a mixed message:
Marilyn Monroe stretched out
in unwinged victory,
pink against red and reaching
not for the president or Nembutal
but because, like cats,
we like to do so.
Someday
like rockets without shells
we'll head for the stars.

On my newly devised calendar
there are only three days a month.
All the rest is space
so that night and day
don't feel uncomfortable
within my confines.
I'm not pushing them around,
making them do this and that.

Just this once
cows are shuffling over the hard rock
of the creekbed.
Two ravens in the black oak
purling whistles, coos, croaks,
raven talk for the dead wild cow's
hindquarter in the grass,
the reddest of reds,
hips crushed when lassoed.
The cow dogs, blue heelers,
first in line for the meat,
all tugging like Africa.
Later, a stray sister
sniffs the femur bone,
bawls in boredom or lament.
In this sun's clock the bone
will become white, whiter, whitest.

The soul's decorum
dissembles
when she understands
that ashes have never
returned to wood.

Even running downstream
I couldn't step
into the same river once
let alone twice.

At first the sound
of the cat drinking water
was unendurable,
then it was broken by a fly
heading north,
a curve bill thrasher
swallowing a red berry,
a dead sycamore leaf
suspended on its way to earth
by a breeze so slight
it went otherwise unnoticed.

The girl in the many-windowed bedroom
with full light coming in from the south
and the sun broken by trees,
has never died.

My friend's great-grandfather
lived from 1798 until 1901.

When a place is finished
you realize it went
like a truly beloved dog
whose vibrance had made
you think it would last forever;
becoming slightly sick,
then well and new again
though older, then sick

again, a long sickness.
A home burial.

They don't appear to have
firmed up their idea when time
started so we can go it alone.
"From birth to old age
it's just you," said Foyan.
So after T'ang foolery and Tancred
(the Black Pope of Umbanda)
I've lived my life in sevens,
not imagining that God could holler,
"Bring me my millennium!"
The sevens are married to each other
by what dogs I owned at the time,
where I fished and hunted,
appealing storms, solstice dinners,
loves and deaths, all the events
that are the marrow of the gods.

O lachrymae sonorense.
From the ground
paced the stars through the ribs
of ocotillo, thin and black
each o'clock till dawn,
rosey but no fingers except
these black thin stalks
directing a billion bright stars,

captured time swelling outward
for us if we are blessed
to be here on the ground,
night sky shot with measured stars,
night sky without end
amen.

NORTH

The mind of which we are unaware is aware of us.

—*R. D. Lang*

The rising sun not beet.
or blood,
but sea-rose red.

I amplified my heartbeat
one thousand times,
the animals at first confused
then decided I was another
thunder being.

While talking directly to god
my attention waxed and waned.
I have a lot on my mind.

I worked out
to make myself as strong
as water.

After all these years
of holding the world together
I let it roll down the hill
into the river.

One tree leads
to another,
walking on
this undescribed earth.

I have dreamed
myself back
to where
I already am.

On a cold day
bear, coyote, cranes.
On a rainy night
a wolf with yellow eyes.
On a windy day
eleven kestrels looking
down at me.
On a hot afternoon
the ravens floated over
where I sunk
myself in the river.

Way out there
in unknown country
I walked at night
to scare myself.

Who is this other,
the secret sharer,
who directs the hand
that twists the heart,
the voice calling out to me
between feather and stone
the hour before dawn?

Somehow
I have turned into
an old brown man
in a green coat.

Having fulfilled
my obligations
my heart moves lightly
to this downward dance.

Bear

Bear died standing up,
paws on log,
howling. Shot
right through the heart.

The hunger only wanted the head,
the hide. I ate her
so she wouldn't go to waste,
dumped naked in a dump,
skinless, looking like ourselves
if we had been flayed,
red as death.

Now there are bear dreams
again for the bear eater: O god,
the bears have come down the hill,
bears from everywhere on earth,
all colors, sizes, filtering
out of the woods behind the cabin.

A half-mile up
I plummeted toward the river to die,
pushed there. Then pinions creaked;
I flew downstream until I clutched
a white pine, the mind stepping back
to see half-bird, half-bear,

waking in the tree to wet
fur and feathers.

Hotei and bear
sitting side by side,
disappear into each other.
Who is to say
which of us is one?

We loaded the thousand-pound logs
by hand, the truck swaying.
Paused to caress my friend and helper,
the bear beside me, eye to eye,
breath breathing breath.

And now tonight, a big blue
November moon. Startled to find myself
wandering the edge of a foggy
tamarack marsh, scenting the cold
wet air, delicious in the moonglow.
Itched against swart hemlock,
an itch to give it all up, shuffling
empty-bellied toward home, the yellow
square of cabin light between trees,
the human shape of yellow light,
to turn around,
to give up again this human shape.

Twilight

For the first time
far in the distance
he could see his twilight
wrapping around the green hill
where three rivers start,
and sliding down toward him
through the trees until it reached
the blueberry marsh and stopped,
telling him to go away, not now,
not for the time being.

Return to Yesenin

For only in praising is my heart still mine,
so violently do I know the world
    —*Rainer Maria Rilke,* "The Sonnets to Orpheus"

I forgot to say that at the moment of death Yesenin
stood there like a misty-eyed pioneer woman trying
to figure out what happened. Were the children
still in the burning barn with the bawling cows?
He was too sensitive for words, and the idea
    of a rope
was a wound he couldn't stop picking at. To step
back from this swinging man twisting clockwise
is to see how we mine ourselves too deeply,
that way down there we can break through
    the soul's
rock into a black underground river that sweeps
    us away.
To be frank, I'd rather live to feed my dogs,
knowing the world says no in ten thousand ways
and yes in only a few. The dogs don't need another
weeping Jesus on the cross of Art, strumming
    the scars
to keep them alive, tending them in a private
garden as if our night-blooming tumors were fruit.
I let you go for twenty years and am now only
checking if you're really dead. There was an urge

to put a few bullets through Nixon's coffin or a big,
sharp wooden stake, and a girl told me she just saw
Jimi Hendrix at an AIDS benefit in Santa Monica.
How could I disbelieve her when her nipples
were rosebuds, though you had to avoid the snakes
in her hair. If you had hung yourself in Argentina
you would have twisted counterclockwise. We can't
ask if it was worth it, can we? Anymore than we can
ask a whale its mother's name. Too bad we couldn't
go to Mexico together and croak a few small gods
back to life. I've entered my third act and am
still following my songs on that thin line between
woods and field, well short of the mouth of
    your hell.

Sonoran Radio
(freely translated)

Looking at a big moon too long
rusts the eyes.

The raped girl stood all day naked
in the cold rain holding a plastic Virgin.
Their colors ran into the ground.

Tonight the Big Dipper poured down
its dark blood into the Sea of Cortez,
El Oso Grande, the hemmoraged bear.

In the supermarket beef feet, chicken feet,
one lone octupus losing its charm.
An old woman named Octavia
who stared at my blind eye
carried out the 100 lb. gunny sack of pintos,
a bag of groceries in the other hand.

Just over the mountains
this other country, despised
and forsaken, makes more sense.
It admits people are complicated,
it tries to ignore its sufferings,
it cheats and loves itself,

it admits God might be made
of stone.

The red bird sits
on the dead brown snake.

The lobo admits its mistake
right after eating
the poisoned calf.

In the forms of death
we are all the same;
destinies are traded
at the very highest levels
in the very high buildings
in clear view of the dump-pickers.

My heart and your heart!

The horses are running from flies.
Twenty-three horses run
around and around from the flies
in the big mesquite *retaque* corral
while five boys watch,
each one smaller
than the next biggest.

In the valley of the Toltecs
the American hunter from Palm Beach
shot one thousand whitewing doves
in a single day, all by himself.

The shark was nearly on shore
when it ate the child in three bites
and the mother kicked the shark in the eye.

The dopers killed the old doctor
in the mountain village,
but then the doctor's patients
stoned the dopers to death,
towing their bodies through town
behind Harley Davidsons.

It is the unpardonable music
stretching the soul
thinner than the skin.
Everyone knows they are not alone
as they suffer the music together
that gives them greater range
for greater suffering.

In the vision
the Virgin who sat in the sycamore
speaks in the voice
of the elegant Trogan,

a bird so rare it goes
mateless for centuries.

The lagoon near the oil refinery
outside Tampico caught fire one night.
Everywhere tarpon were jumping
higher than a basketball hoop,
covered with oily flames,
the gill plates rattling,
throwing off burning oil.

The black dove and white dove
intermarried, producing not brown doves,
but some white doves and black doves.
Down the line, however,
born in our garden a deep yellow dove
more brilliant than gold
and blind as a bat.
She sits on my shoulder
cooing night songs in the day,
sleeping a few minutes at noon
and always at midnight, wakes
as if from a nightmare
screaming "Guadalupe!"

She said that outside Magdalena
on a mountainside
she counted thirteen guitarists

perched just below a cave
from which they tried to evoke
the usual flow
of blood and flowers.

Up in the borderland mountains
the moon fell slowly on Animas Peak
until it hit it directly
and broke like an egg,
spilling milk on the talus
and scree, sliding in a flood
through a dozen canyons.
The wind rose to fifty knots,
burning the moon
deep into the skin.

In a seaside restaurant
in Puerto Vallarta
a Bosnian woman killed a Serbian man
with a dinner fork,
her big arm pumping the tines
like a jackhammer
before the frightened diners
who decided not to believe it.
She escaped the police net,
fleeing into the green mountains,
fork in hand.

The preying mantis crawled
up the left nostril of our burro
and killed it.

Nightjars and goat suckers,
birds from the far edge of twilight
carrying ghosts from place to place,
just hitching a ride, the ghosts
say to the birds, slapping
on the harness of black thread.
Even in *el norte* the whippoorwill's
nest is lined with the gossamer thread
of this ghost harness.

The cow dogs
tore apart
and ate
the pregnant housecat.
The grey hawk
(only twenty pair left in the U.S.)
flew close over
the vermillion flycatcher
perched on the tip
of the green juniper tree.
The waitress in the diner
where I ate my menudo
told me that Christ actually

bled to death. Back in those days
nails were the same as railroad spikes,
and the sun was hot as hell.
She sees the Resurrection
without irony or backspin.
"We are so lucky," she said.
"I couldn't live with all the things
I've done wrong in my life.
I feel better when I'm forgiven."

His dog sneezed
and crawled under a pickup
to get away from the sun.
The guitar and concertina music
swept down the mountainside
from the old cowboy's funeral,
hat and bridle
hanging from a white cross
in a cluster of admirable
plastic flowers.

The ravens are waiting
in the oak at twilight
for the coyotes to come
and open up the dead steer.
The ravens can't break through
cowhide with their beaks
and have been there since dawn

eager for the coyotes to get things started.
There's plenty for everyone.

These black beetles,
big as a thumb
are locked in dead embrace
either in love or rage.

The bull does not want
to be caught. For five
hours and as many miles
on a hot morning
three cowboys and a half-dozen
cowdogs have worked
the bull toward the pen.
The truck is ready to take
him to the sale. He's known
as a baloney bull, inferring
his destiny: old, used up,
too lazy and tired to mount cows.
Meanwhile he's bawling, blowing
snot, charging, hooking a horn
at the horses, dogs, a stray tree.
Finally loaded, I said goodbye
to his blood-red eyes.
He rumbles, raises his huge neck
and bawls at the sun.

The cowdog licks her cancerous
and bloated teats.
Otherwise, she's the happiest
dog I know, always smiling,
always trying to help out.

I gave the woman seven roses
and she smiled, holding
the bouquet a couple of hours
at dusk before saying goodbye.
The next day I gave her
a brown calf and three chickens
and she took me to bed.
Over her shoulder a rose
petal fell for an hour.

From a thicket full
of red cardinals
burst seven black javelinas,
including three infants
the size of housecats.

There were so many birds
at the mountain spring
they drove one insane
at dawn and twilight;
bushes clotted with birds
like vulgar Christmas trees.

I counted thirteen hundred
of a hundred different kinds,
all frozen in place
when the grey hawk flew by,
its keening voice
the precise weight of death.

Magdalena kept taking off her clothes
for hours until there was nothing left,
not even a trace of moisture on the leather chair.
Perhaps it was because
she was a government employee
and had lost a child.
It was the sleight of her hand.
I never saw her again.

Another bowl of menudo
and she's on a rampage in a black
Guadalupe T-shirt: "We can't keep
working through the used part every day.
Everyone is tired of dope. Day in, day out,
the newspapers are full of dope news,
people are shot dead and not so dead,
sent to prison, and both police and criminals
are so bored with dope they weep
day and night, going about their jobs,
living and dying for this stupid dope.
There has to be more than dope. Understand?"

I dreamed here
before I arrived.
Chuck and whirr
of elf owls above firelight,
dozens in the black oak
staring down into the fire
beyond which a thousand white sycamore
limbs move their legs into the night.
Sonoran moon gets red
again as she sets in the dust
we've colored with blood.

For a complete list, please visit www.shambhala.com.

SHAMBHALA POCKET LIBRARY

AFTER IKKYŪ
Jim Harrison

THE ART OF PEACE
Morihei Ueshiba

BECOME WHAT YOU ARE
Alan Watts

THE BODHISATTVA GUIDE
His Holiness the Fourteenth Dalai Lama

THE BOOK OF TEA
Kakuzo Okakura

THE CLOUD OF UNKNOWING
Translated by Carmen Acevedo Butcher

THE DHAMMAPADA
Translated and edited by Gil Fronsdal

I CHING
Translated by Thomas Cleary